You Had Me at Pie!

FRUIT, CUSTARD, MERINGUE & MORE FROM KITCHEN CONSERVATORY

Anne Carpenter

Reedy Press
PO Box 5131
St. Louis, MO 63139
www.reedypress.com

Design: Richard Roden

All cover and interior photos are courtesy of Julia Calleo.

ISBN: 9781681065403

Printed in the United States

24 25 26 27 28 5 4 3 2 1

CONTENTS

INTRODUCTION

The answer is, "Yes, of course I want a piece of pie!" Pie is seduction. Pie is comfort. No one turns down pie, and homemade pie with home-made crust is the best. You had me at pie.

One student, Fred, who took a pie class of mine several years ago, reported back that he had made over 80 "comfort" pies that he has delivered to sick and bereaved friends. He became the pie man with his comfort pies—and no comfort tastes better than a homemade pie.

The secret to the most delicious pie is in the crust. This cookbook teaches how to make the ultimate crust that is both flaky and tender. Yes, you can make homemade pie dough! These techniques are radical: bigger chunks of fat, a high ratio of fat to flour, and very little water. This dough is not picture-perfect, but the taste of the finished pie crust is incomparable. The pie crust is so scrumptious that some eaters think the filling is superfluous!

The best pie crust is made with a combination of butter (for flavor) and shortening (for tenderness).

I love pie, and I want everyone to enjoy freshly-baked pie with homemade crust. I have made and baked thousands of pies, and I have taught hundreds of students how to make and bake pie in many cooking classes.

Pie is not a fancy dessert, but given the choice between eating pie or cake, I choose pie. Pie does not need to be artful; the best pies are humble.

What's your favorite pie to eat? My favorite pie is cherry. It is worth driving to Wisconsin in July to source fresh Montmorency cherries, which are the best cherries for pie filling. I do love all the double-crusted fruit pies, and my basic fruit pie filling can be adapted to other fruits: rhubarb, strawberry-rhubarb, blackberry, mixed berries, gooseberry, or apricot.

Start your ovens and start baking better pies!

Perfect Pie Dough: Flaky and Tender

A pie dough made with only butter is flaky and delicious. A pie dough made with only shortening or lard is meltingly tender. Use both butter and shortening for a perfect pie. Pie dough is a "short" crust, which means that it has a high ratio of fat to flour and that the gluten in the flour is cut by the chunks of fat in the dough. When the cold dough is baked in a hot oven, the cold fat melts in the dough and creates flaky pastry. A short pastry dough should be both flaky and tender.

TIPS FOR PERFECT PIE

1. **Cold dough.** The refrigerator is the pie-maker's best friend. Use cold butter, ice water, and refrigerate the dough for 20 minutes before rolling out. At no time should the dough just sit out on the countertop. Work quickly in rolling out the dough so that the dough does not dawdle before baking.
2. **Bigger chunks of fat.** Many recipes call for mixing the fat into the flour until it looks like coarse crumbs. Cut the fat only until the pieces are dime-sized, not pebbles. Why? Because the visible chunks of cold fat will pop in the hot oven and produce a flakier pastry. The dough should look marbleized with chunks of fat.
3. **Equal parts of butter and shortening.** To make a crust both tender and flaky, use butter for taste and flakiness and shortening for tenderness. An all-butter crust will never be tender and an all-shortening crust will be short on flavor.

4. **Don't overhandle the dough.** Anyone who bakes bread wants to knead the dough. Kneading the dough develops the gluten in the flour, which will toughen the crust. There is no need to make the dough look beautiful. A shaggy dough will bake into a better tasting crust.

5. **Do not use a machine.** A food processor or stand mixer will overmix the dough and warm up the butter.

6. **Just enough water.** The amount of water added to the dough will always vary. Add just enough, since adding too much water produces a wet dough, which will require more flour to roll out. Better to leave a few dry crumbs in the bottom of the bowl than to add more water.

7. **Wrap the dough.** The ball of dough should be very tightly wrapped in plastic wrap before refrigerating. The tight wrap helps the liquid to hydrate the flour.

8. **Flour does not add flavor.** Adding too much flour changes the ratio of fat-to-flour and takes away flavor. After all, fat is flavor! I use a ratio of 1 cup flour to 1/2 cup fat, which is a really high ratio. So rolling out such a fatty dough can be very sticky. A cold dough is less sticky. Do use plenty of flour when rolling out the dough. Sprinkle flour on the dough, not on the rolling pin. Remember to brush off all excess flour before fitting the dough into the pie plate.

9. **Brush with egg wash.** Combine 1 egg yolk with one tablespoon water. Brush the egg wash on the top crust, but do not brush the pie edges, which can overbake. An egg wash produces a golden brown and shiny crust.

10. **Do not use flour in fruit pie fillings.** Flour tastes pasty and does not thicken well. Potato starch is flavorless and thickens well. Second choice is cornstarch. A pie with 6 cups of fruit (3 pounds) needs 3 tablespoons of starch.

11. **Look for browning and bubbling.** Fruit pies are finished baking when the top crust is brown and the juices are bubbling up. When the juice is boiling, then the fruit, sugar, and starch have combined to thicken the pie filling.

12. **Pie is best eaten the day it is baked.** Pastry loses flavor and texture when stored in the refrigerator, although leftover pie does make for an excellent breakfast!

Tools for Pie Making

- Pastry Blender
- Gravy Separator
- Silicone Rolling Mat
- Rolling Pin
- Bench Knife
- Flour Duster
- Pie Plate
- Pastry Brush
- Ceramic Pie Weights
- Sieve
- Microplane Zester
- Food Processor
- Stand Mixer
- Torch
- Candy Thermometer

PERFECT PIE DOUGH

2 cups (9 ounces) all-purpose flour

¾ teaspoon salt

2 tablespoons sugar

8 tablespoons butter

8 tablespoons Crisco shortening

Ice water as needed, about 4 tablespoons

Mix together the flour, salt, and sugar. Use a pastry blender to cut the butter into the flour until dime-sized. Then cut in the shortening. Fill a gravy separator (which pours from the bottom) with ice and water. Add just enough ice water to moisten the dough and use one hand to pull the dough into a ball against the side of the bowl. Wrap the dough tightly in plastic wrap and refrigerate for 20 minutes.

Cut the dough in half. Sprinkle a large silicone pastry mat with flour and roll out the dough to fit the bottom of a 9-inch pie plate. Place the pie plate on the mat to secure and then use the pastry mat to flip the dough into the pie plate. Fill the pie plate with fruit, then roll out the top crust and fit on top of the fruit. To crimp the edges, pull the dough together and squeeze to form a border. Use a fork or fingers to shape the edge.

TO BLIND BAKE PIE

1 cup (4 ½ ounces) all-purpose flour

¼ teaspoon salt

1 tablespoon sugar

4 tablespoons butter

4 tablespoons Crisco shortening

Ice water as needed, about 2 tablespoons

6 cups ceramic pie weights

Mix together the flour, salt, and sugar. Use a pastry blender to cut the butter into the flour until dime-sized. Then cut in the shortening. Add just enough ice water to moisten the dough and use one hand to pull the dough into a ball. Wrap the dough tightly in plastic wrap. Refrigerate for 20 minutes. Sprinkle the silicone mat with flour and roll out the dough to fit the bottom of a 9-inch pie plate.

Place the dough in a pie plate, cover with aluminum foil, and fill with pie weights. Be sure to use enough pie weights to fill the whole pan so that the sides of the pie dough do not collapse. Bake at 375 degrees for 20 minutes. Remove the pie plate from the oven, then carefully remove the foil and pie weights. Return the pie to the oven and bake for 5 more minutes. Remove and let cool completely before adding the filling.

Baking "blind" is to pre-bake a crust for a cold filling. Use ceramic pie weights to create a cavity that can be filled after the crust cools. Pie weights provide both volume to fill the cavity plus weight to keep the bottom crust from rising.

GRAHAM CRACKER PIE CRUST

½ recipe Perfect Pie dough

½ cup graham cracker crumbs, or as needed

Sprinkle the pastry rolling mat with graham cracker crumbs. Place the cold dough on top and sprinkle with crumbs. Roll out the dough in the crumbs, adding more as needed. Use the pastry mat to turn the dough into the pie plate. Crimp the edges. Fill with a filling or bake blind for a cold filling. (Note: this dough does not work well with a top crust.)

1

2

3

4

5

6

Let's face it: a graham cracker crust is boring because there is no pastry! But what is really delicious is a combination of pie dough with graham crackers. Using the dry graham crackers makes rolling out the pie dough really easy. I love this crust with lemon and pumpkin pies.

Graham Cracker Pie Crust

Double Crusted Fruit Pies

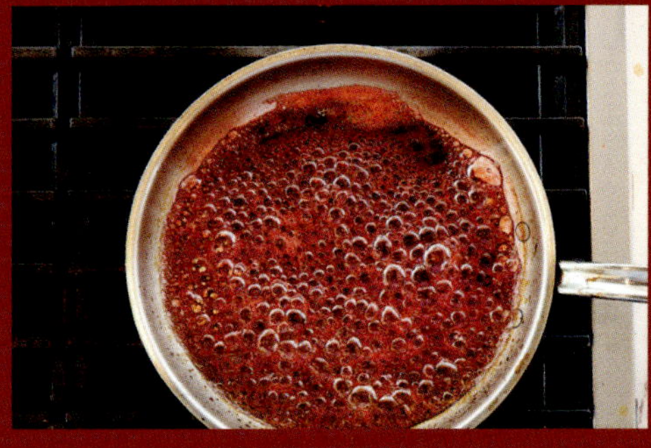

The secret to a great fruit filling is to concentrate the flavor of the fruit. Let the fruit (particularly apple and cherry) sit in sugar for several hours. Then drain the juice and place the juice in a sauce pan. Boil the juice until reduced to half or two-thirds of the original volume. This process removes the water from the fruit filling and concentrates the fruit taste. The result is a pie filling that is amazing!

Note: *Do not do this step with blueberries or blackberries, as they do not have enough liquid.*

Tip!

In general, apples that are good for eating are not good for baking, because eating apples are generally too sweet. Choose tart apples for a tastier pie filling, but I find that green apples still taste green after baking.

Apple Pie

APPLE

6 cups (3 pounds) peeled, cored, and sliced apples (Jonathon, McIntosh, Jonagold, or Golden Delicious)

½ cup white sugar

3 tablespoons potato starch

¼ cup brown sugar

1 tablespoon lemon juice

1 teaspoon cinnamon

½ teaspoon nutmeg

2 tablespoons butter

Egg wash: one egg yolk mixed with 1 tablespoon water

1 recipe Perfect Pie Dough

Mix together the apples and white sugar. Let sit for at least 2 hours and up to 24 hours at room temperature. Strain the juice and place the juice in a sauce pan. Bring to a boil and reduce to one-third of the volume. The liquid will be very syrupy.

In a separate bowl, mix the apples with the potato starch. Then mix in brown sugar, reduced juice, lemon, and seasonings. Place the bottom dough in a pie plate. Pour in the apples. Dot the top with butter. Cover with the top dough. Crimp the edges. Brush the top of the pie dough with an egg wash, but do not brush the edges. Bake at 375 degrees for 45 minutes.

BLUEBERRY

6 cups washed and stemmed blueberries

3 tablespoons potato starch

¾ cup sugar

Zest of one lemon

2 tablespoons butter

Egg wash: one egg yolk mixed with 1 tablespoon water

1 recipe Perfect Pie Dough

Mix together the berries and starch. Fold in sugar and zest. Pour in the bottom dough. Dot the top with butter. Cover with the top dough. Crimp the edges. Brush the center of the pie dough with an egg wash. Bake at 375 degrees for 45 minutes.

CHERRY

Mix together the cherries and sugar. Let sit for an hour, then strain the juice and place in a fry pan. Bring the juice to a boil and cook until reduced to one-quarter of the original volume. Add the sugar syrup back to the fruit and stir in the starch and rum. Pour in the bottom dough. Dot the top with butter. Cover with the top dough. Crimp the edges. Brush the pie dough (but not the edge) with an egg wash. Bake at 375 degrees for 45 minutes.

6 cups pitted sour or Montmorency cherries

¾ cup sugar

3 tablespoons potato starch

1 tablespoon rum

2 tablespoons butter

Egg wash: one egg yolk mixed with 1 tablespoon water

1 recipe Perfect Pie Dough

Tip!

The sweet Bing or Rainier cherries do not make a good pie filling because the fruit is not soft enough. Pie cherries are small, tart, and soft enough that they can be pitted by just squeezing the fruit. Tart cherries are available fresh in June and July. If using frozen cherries, be sure to defrost completely and drain the excess liquid, which can be used to make the boiled-down syrup for the pie.

PEACH

Mix together the peaches and starch. Fold in sugar, ginger, and rum. Pour in the bottom dough. Dot the top with butter. Cover with the top dough. Crimp the edges. Brush the pie dough (not the edges) with an egg wash. Bake at 375 degrees for 45 minutes.

6 cups (3 pounds) peeled and pitted ripe peaches

3 tablespoons potato starch

¾ cup sugar

1 teaspoon ground ginger

1 tablespoon rum

2 tablespoons butter

Egg wash: one egg yolk mixed with 1 tablespoon water

1 recipe Perfect Pie Dough

Tip!

To peel peaches, bring a pot of water to a boil. Cook the peaches for 10 seconds, then remove with a slotted spoon. The skins can then be easily removed.

RAISIN

2 cups apple cider

2 cups sugar

1 ½ pounds apples, peeled, cored, and chopped

½ pound Concord grapes, skins popped and saved and seeds removed

1 cup currants

1 cup golden raisins

Zest of one lemon

¼ cup chopped candied citron or the zest of one orange

¾ teaspoon salt

¼ teaspoon each ground cinnamon, allspice, and mace

¼ cup bourbon

1 recipe Perfect Pie Dough

Place the apple cider in a large saucepan, bring to a boil, and cook until reduced to 1 cup. Then add sugar, apples, grapes, currants, raisins, zest, citron, salt, spices, and bourbon. Bring to a boil, then simmer, stirring occasionally, for about 30 minutes, until the mixture is cooked and reduced by half. Cool. Pour into a pie dough and cover with a top crust. Bake at 350 degrees for 40 minutes.

Candied citron lends a floral taste to the filling. Citron looks like a bumpy lemon with no juice and is available fresh in the winter months, but the rind must be cooked in sugar before using in recipes.

CONCORD GRAPE

Remove the stems from the grapes and wash. Squeeze each grape to pop the skins off, and reserve the skins. Place the grape pulp in a food processor and puree. Strain to remove the seeds and discard the seeds. Combine the grape juice with the grape skins. Stir in the starch, sugar, and zest. Pour into a pie dough and dot the top with butter. Carefully place the top dough on the filling and crimp the edges. (The filling will be quite liquid, but it will set in baking.) Brush the dough with the egg wash (do not egg wash the edge of the pie). Bake at 375 degrees for 45 minutes, or until the filling is bubbly and the top is browned.

6 cups Concord grapes

3 tablespoons potato starch

¾ cup sugar

Zest of one orange

2 tablespoons butter

Egg wash: one egg yolk mixed with 1 tablespoon water

1 recipe Perfect Pie Dough

Fresh Concord grapes are only available in August and September. Each grape needs to be squeezed to remove the seeds, but this pie is worth the effort once a year!

Tip!

The white part, or pith, of the lemon is very bitter. Be sure to use only the yellow part of the skin, then completely remove the white pith before cutting up the fruit.

SHAKER LEMON

4 lemons

2 cups sugar

1 teaspoon salt

4 eggs

1 recipe Perfect Pie Dough

Using a Microplane grater, zest the lemons and reserve. Cut the ends off of the lemons and then use a thin knife to cut off the bitter pith (the white part of the rind). Slice the lemons very thinly and remove any seeds. Mix the lemon pulp with the sugar, lemon zest, and salt. Beat in the eggs and pour into a pie plate fitted with dough for a bottom crust. Roll out the other half of the dough and place on top of the lemons. Crimp the dough together. Brush the top with an egg wash and bake at 350 degrees for 45 minutes.

Custard Pies

There are two types of custard pies: baked and stovetop. The Banana Cream and Chocolate pies are stovetop custards that are chilled, then poured into a pre-baked pie crust. The Buttermilk, Maple, and Pumpkin pies are oven-baked custards.

Buttermilk-Berry Pie

Buttermilk Pie with Two Variations

Each one is so good that I could not decide which one to include!

BUTTERMILK-BERRY

VARIATION 1

Mix together the butter and sugar until light and fluffy. Add the egg yolks, flour, lemon, nutmeg, and salt. Fold in the buttermilk. Whip the egg whites to soft peaks and fold into the batter. Sprinkle the berries on the bottom of the crust and spoon the batter on top. Bake at 325 degrees for 45 minutes, or until the pie shakes like jello. Do not overbake; the pie will completely set when cool.

- 6 tablespoons butter, at room temperature
- 1 cup sugar
- 3 eggs, separated
- ¼ cup flour
- Zest and juice of one lemon
- ¼ teaspoon freshly grated nutmeg
- ¼ teaspoon salt
- 1 cup buttermilk
- 6 ounces fresh raspberries or blueberries
- ½ recipe Perfect Pie Dough

BUTTERMILK-BOURBON

VARIATION 2

- 6 tablespoons butter, at room temperature
- 1 cup sugar
- 3 eggs, separated
- ¼ cup flour
- ¼ teaspoon freshly grated nutmeg
- ¼ teaspoon salt
- 1 cup buttermilk
- ¼ cup bourbon
- ½ recipe Perfect Pie Dough

Mix together the butter and sugar. Add the egg yolks, flour, nutmeg, and salt. Fold in the buttermilk and bourbon. Whip the egg whites to soft peaks and fold into the batter. Spoon the batter on top. Bake at 325 degrees for 45 minutes, or until the pie shakes like jello. Do not overbake; the pie will completely set when cool.

MAPLE SYRUP CUSTARD

Mix together the sugars, flour, cinnamon, salt, vinegar, and cream. Pour into a pie dough fitted into a pie plate.

Bake at 400 degrees for 45 minutes. The pie will still be jiggly when you remove it from the oven. Let cool completely before serving.

- ½ cup maple syrup
- ½ cup brown sugar
- ¼ cup flour
- 1 teaspoon cinnamon
- ¼ teaspoon salt
- 1 tablespoon apple cider vinegar
- 1½ cups heavy cream
- ½ recipe Perfect Pie Dough

“PUMPKIN”

- 1 butternut squash, about 2-3 pounds
- 1 cup sugar
- 2 teaspoons cinnamon
- ½ teaspoon ground ginger
- ½ teaspoon ground nutmeg
- 1 teaspoon vanilla extract
- 3 eggs
- ¾ cup heavy cream
- ½ recipe Perfect Pie Dough

To prepare the squash, cut in half lengthwise, scoop out the seeds and roast at 350 degrees skin-side-up on a lined sheet pan until tender, about an hour. Remove and discard the skin. Alternatively, peel and dice the squash and steam in a vegetable steamer until tender, about 20 minutes. Pass the squash through a ricer or use a food processor for a smooth consistency.

Place the squash in a saucepan with the sugar and cook over medium heat until any liquid from the squash has evaporated and the squash is drier, about 20 minutes. Frequently stir the squash so it does not brown. Remove from heat when the squash is no longer wet.

Measure out 2 cups of squash-sugar mixture and whisk with spices, eggs, and cream. The filling can be made 2 days ahead of time and kept in the refrigerator before pouring into the pie dough.

Pour the batter into the pie plate fitted with a bottom dough and bake at 350 degrees for 50-60 minutes. The pie can be served warm or cold. Serve with whipped cream.

Variation: Pumpkin Chiffon Pie

Follow the same recipe, but separate the eggs. Mix the yolks with the squash, spices, and cream. In a separate bowl, whip the whites until stiff peaks form. Gently fold the whites into the squash batter. Bake immediately and serve hot from the oven with whipped cream.

A fresh butternut squash makes a more delicious pie than a canned filling. Let this be our secret and tell your guests that they are eating pumpkin pie – the best pumpkin pie they ever ate!

CHOCOLATE CUSTARD

Custard

Heat the cream in a saucepan. In a separate bowl, whisk together the yolks, salt, and sugar until the mixture is pale and thick. Fold in the starch. Temper the yolk mixture by whisking in some of the hot cream, then pour the yolks into the saucepan. Cook over medium heat, whisking constantly, until the cream boils. Remove from heat, add chocolate, and let the hot liquid melt the chocolate. Cool completely, then pour into the baked crust. Top the chilled chocolate custard with Italian meringue (page 18) or whipped cream (page 25).

2 cups half-and-half

6 egg yolks

Dash of salt

⅔ cup sugar

3 tablespoons corn starch

4 ounces bittersweet chocolate

1 recipe Blind-Baked Pie Dough

BANANA CREAM

2 cups half-and-half

1 vanilla bean, split in half lengthwise

6 egg yolks

Dash of salt

⅔ cup sugar

3 tablespoons corn starch

Custard

Heat the cream with the vanilla bean in a saucepan. In a separate bowl, whisk together the yolks, salt, and sugar until the mixture is pale and thick. Fold in the starch. Temper the yolk mixture by whisking in some of the hot cream, then pour the yolks into the saucepan. Cook over medium heat, whisking constantly, until the cream boils. Remove from heat and cool.

1 recipe Blind-Baked Pie Dough

2 bananas, peeled and sliced

Crust and Bananas

Place the bananas on top of the baked pie crust. Top with custard. Pipe the meringue on top of the cream. Use a culinary torch to brown the meringue.

Italian Meringue (recipe on pg. 18)

LEMON MERINGUE

3 eggs

3 egg yolks

1¼ cups sugar

Zest of one lemon

¾ cup lemon juice

10 tablespoons cold butter, cut into pieces

1 recipe Blind-Baked Pie Dough

Filling

In a saucepan, combine the eggs, egg yolks, sugar, zest, and lemon juice and whisk well. Whisk the mixture and cook until thickened. Strain. Remove from heat and whisk in the butter. Chill until completely cold, and then pour into the baked pie crust.

1 cup sugar

4 egg whites

Italian Meringue

Combine the sugar with ¼ cup water in a small saucepan. Clip a candy thermometer on the pan. Cook until the syrup reaches 238 degrees. When the sugar is close to the temperature, start whipping the egg whites in a stand mixer on high speed. Very slowly, pour the hot sugar syrup into the whites. When finished adding the syrup, turn off the mixer and place the meringue in a pastry bag fitted with a large star tip. Pipe the meringue on top of the filling. Alternatively, dollop the meringue on top of the lemon filling and use the back of a spoon to swirl the meringue. Use a culinary torch to brown the meringue. Chill the pie before serving.

Cool the pie crust, lemon filling, and meringue before assembling the pie. A warm filling will be a runny pie.

Lemon Meringue

Strawberry Meringue

STRAWBERRY MERINGUE

½ cup strawberry jam

2 tablespoons Framboise or Chambord liqueur

1 quart strawberries, hulled and sliced

1 recipe Blind-Baked Pie Dough

Strawberries

Place the jam and framboise in a sauce pan on medium heat and stir until smooth. Toss the jam with the strawberries and place in the pie crust.

1 cup half-and-half

½ vanilla bean, split lengthwise

3 egg yolks

⅓ cup sugar

1½ tablespoons potato or corn starch

Crème Chiboust

To make the pastry cream, heat the half-and-half. In a separate bowl, beat the yolks with the sugar and a dash of salt until pale and ribbony. Add the starch. Temper the yolks with a little of the hot cream. Pour the yolk mixture into the sauce pan and cook over medium heat, stirring constantly, until the mixture thickens. Remove the vanilla bean.

4 egg whites (1/2 cup)

1 cup sugar

¼ cup water

Meringue

To make the meringue, combine a cup of sugar in a sauce pan and bring to a boil. Use a candy thermometer and continue boiling until the temperature reaches 238 degrees. Whip the egg whites in a stand electric mixer until stiff. Carefully and very slowly, pour the sugar syrup into the whites and continue beating until the whites have cooled.

Fold the pastry cream into the meringue. Use a pastry bag fitted with a plain tip and pipe the chiboust on top of the strawberries. Brown the meringue with a torch.

What's better than a meringue topping? Creme Chiboust is a yummy combination of meringue and custard. Use a torch to brown the topping.

Transparent Pies

Transparent is the name of pie fillings that are set with eggs but have no cream.

CHESS

- ½ cup butter, at room temperature
- 1½ cups sugar
- 1½ tablespoons cornmeal
- 3 eggs
- 3 tablespoons lemon juice
- 2 teaspoons lemon zest
- 1 teaspoon vanilla extract
- ⅛ teaspoon salt
- ½ recipe Perfect Pie Dough

Mix together the butter and sugar until smooth and fluffy. Beat in the cornmeal, eggs, lemon juice and zest, vanilla, salt, and blend well. Fit a pie dough into a pie plate and pour in the filling. Bake at 350 degrees for 35 to 40 minutes. Cool completely before serving.

MAPLE NUT CIDER

Place the apple cider in a sauce pan, bring to a boil, and cook until the liquid is reduced to ¼-cup. Cool. Blend together the sugar, butter, eggs, salt, syrup, and reduced cider. Place the nuts in the bottom of the pie plate fitted with pie dough. Pour the filling over the nuts. Bake at 350 degrees for 45 minutes, or until the filling is set. Cool before serving.

- 2 cups apple cider
- 1 cup maple or brown sugar
- 4 tablespoons butter, melted
- 4 eggs
- ¼ teaspoon salt
- 1 cup maple syrup
- 2 cups walnuts or pecans
- ½ recipe Perfect Pie Dough

PECAN

With variations for Chocolate-Pecan, Cherry-Pecan, or Chocolate-Cherry-Pecan

1 cup brown sugar

4 tablespoons butter, melted

4 eggs

¼ teaspoon salt

1 teaspoon vanilla extract

1 cup corn syrup

2 tablespoons rum or bourbon

½ cup chocolate chips and/or dried cherries (optional)

2 cups pecans

½ recipe Perfect Pie Dough

Roll out a pie dough and fit into the bottom of a pie plate. Layer the chocolate and/or cherries on top of the dough and then add the pecans. Whisk together the sugar, butter, eggs, salt, vanilla, syrup, and rum. Pour the filling over the pecans. Bake at 350 degrees for an hour or until the filling has set.

Tip!

If using chocolate chips and/or dried fruit, add them first to the pie plate, then top with pecans. The chocolate and fruit will burn if they are on top of the pecans in the pie.

Chocolate Pies

French Silk

FRENCH SILK

Filling

In a double boiler, melt the chocolate and remove from the heat. In a stand mixer, mix together the butter and sugar until light and fluffy, about 10 minutes. Do not under-mix! Then blend in the chocolate and vanilla. Add the eggs to the mixer and mix very well. Pour into the pre-baked pie shell and chill.

4 ounces unsweetened chocolate

1 cup butter, at room temperature

1½ cups extra-fine or caster sugar

1 teaspoon vanilla

4 eggs

1 recipe Blind-Baked Pie Dough

Topping

Whip the cream, sugar, and vanilla to soft peaks. Do not over whip. Use a pastry bag to pipe the cream onto the chocolate filling. Garnish with chocolate shavings.

2 cups heavy cream

¼ cup powdered sugar

1 tablespoon vanilla extract

Chocolate shavings for garnish

CHOCOLATE ANGEL

4 egg whites (½ cup egg whites)

¼ teaspoon salt

¼ teaspoon cream of tartar

1 cup sugar

1 teaspoon vanilla extract

Crust

Place the egg whites in the bowl of a stand mixer and add the salt and cream of tartar. Whip on high until the whites hold soft peaks. Add the sugar, one tablespoon at a time, until the whites are glossy and stiff. Add the vanilla. Spoon into a pastry bag fitted with a plain tip. On a parchment-lined cookie sheet, pipe 4-inch circles of meringue and then pipe an extra layer on the edge of the meringue to make individual pie shells. Bake at 275 for 45 minutes, or until the meringue is dry and golden brown. Let cool completely.

½ pound bittersweet chocolate

½ cup butter

4 eggs, separated

1 tablespoon sugar

½ cup heavy cream

Filling

Melt butter and chocolate in a double boiler. Whip egg yolks with a pinch of salt and stir into the chocolate until smooth. Whip egg whites until soft peaks form, sprinkle with sugar, and whip until glossy. Fold into chocolate mixture. Whip the cream until soft peaks form and then fold into chocolate mixture. Do not overmix. Use a pastry bag fitted with a plain tip and pipe the filling high into the cooled meringue shells. Refrigerate until firm.

Tip!

This cobbler has a crisp, cookie-like crust. Since everyone wants some of the topping, be sure to bake in a wide, shallow pan.

Peach Cobbler

APPLE BROWN BETTY

Combine the breadcrumbs and butter. Mix together the apples with the sugar, salt, cinnamon, nutmeg, cloves, and lemon. Layer one-third of the breadcrumbs on the bottom of a baking dish. Top with half of the apples, then another third of the breadcrumbs. Repeat. Cover with foil and bake at 350 degrees for 30 minutes. Uncover and brown the topping at 400 degrees for 15 minutes.

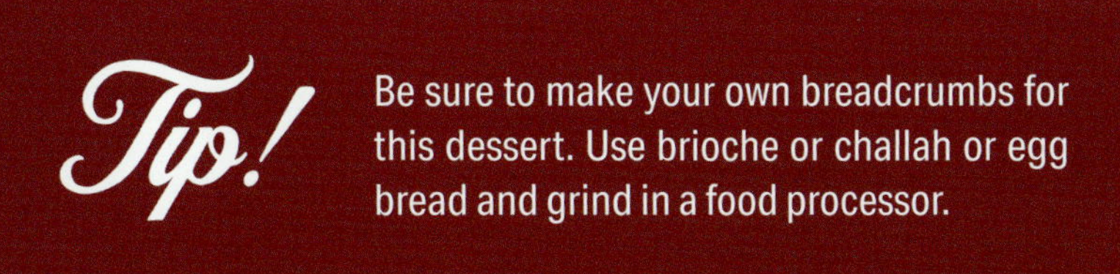

Be sure to make your own breadcrumbs for this dessert. Use brioche or challah or egg bread and grind in a food processor.

3 cups fresh breadcrumbs (enriched bread such as brioche)

12 tablespoons butter, melted

8 Jonathon apples, peeled, cored, and sliced

1⅓ cups brown sugar

¼ teaspoon salt

1 teaspoon cinnamon

½ teaspoon freshly grated nutmeg

½ teaspoon ground cloves

Zest and juice of one lemon

FRUIT COBBLER

Fruit

Toss the fruit with the sugar and starch and place in a baking dish (at least 9×13 inches).

12 cups prepared fruit (peeled and pitted stoned fruits or berries or a combination)

1 tablespoon potato or corn starch

½ cup sugar

Topping

Mix together the butter and sugar until creamy and well-mixed. Stir in the egg. Mix together the flour, salt, and baking powder. Fold into the butter mixture. The dough will be very soft. Drop mounds of dough on top of the prepared fruit. Bake at 375 degrees for 40 to 45 minutes, until browned and crispy on top.

1 cup butter, at room temperature

1 cup sugar

1 egg

1 cup flour

¼ teaspoon salt

½ teaspoon baking powder

Pumpkin Chiffon Pie